# ACCI DENT ISM

# Josef Frank

Mikael Bergquist  Olof Michélsen

BIRKHÄUSER

Basel

EDITORS: Mikael Bergquist, Olof Michélsen, Stockholm
LAYOUT/GRAPHIC DESIGN: Daniel Bjugård, Stockholm
MODELS: Modellverkstaden, Stockholm
PHOTO MODELS: Magnus Östh – Studio Lindman, Stockholm
TRANSLATION INTO ENGLISH: Ruth Kvarnström-Jones, Stockholm

Library of Congress Cataloging-in-Publication data
A CIP catalog record for this book has been applied for at the Library
of Congress.

Bibliographic information published by the German National Library
The German National Library lists this publication in the Deutsche
Nationalbibliografie; detailed bibliographic data are available on the
Internet at http://dnb.dnb.de.

© 2016 Birkhäuser Verlag GmbH, Basel
P.O. Box 44, 4009 Basel, Switzerland
Part of Walter de Gruyter GmbH, Berlin/Boston

Printed on acid-free paper produced from chlorine-free pulp. TCF ∞
Printed in Germany
ISBN 978-3-0356-1119-9

9 8 7 6 5 4 3 2 1
www.birkhauser.com

# CONTENTS

# ACCIDENTISM: JOSEF FRANK
*Mikael Bergquist  Olof Michélsen*

**"Beauty today can have no other measure except the depth to which a work of art resolves contradictions. A work of art must cut through the contradictions and overcome them, not by covering them up, but by pursuing them."**
**Theodor W. Adorno, 1965**

**"Every great work of art must border on kitsch."**
**Josef Frank**

## Panorama

The final meeting of the CIAM – Congrès Internationaux d'Architecture Moderne – was held in 1959. Modernism was suddenly old-fashioned. The pioneers from the 1920s and 30s were now all old men. The heroic period was definitively over. The west was being inundated with "mediocre modernism", with constant self-repetition and increasingly diluted and pale copies. "C'est du mauvais Corbu," answered Le Corbusier when asked what he thought of Marcel Breuer's plan for the UNESCSO build-

4

Delegates at the first CIAM conference, La Sarraz, Switzerland, 1928.
Josef Frank far right.

ing in Paris. Modernism had largely developed into the rigidified format that so many predecessors had predicted and warned of as far back as the 1920s.

But a young generation of architects in Europe and the USA were questioning the codes, aesthetics and strict morals of modernism from a number of different directions. Architects such as Smithsons, Cedric Price, Venturi/Scott Brown were fascinated, instead, by the ordinary, the ugly, the everyday. From the wreckage of CIAM arose Team X. In the 1960s, the criticism would culminate in a multitude of new movements and counter-movements in Italy, Holland, Austria, France, the UK and Japan.

Already in the early 1950s, a heated architectural debate was taking place in Germany, involving a settling of accounts with the ideals of the Bauhaus school. Bauhaus was still synonymous with modern architecture and the successes of its old teachers in the USA had brought about a rejuvenation of the school in the post-war period.

A variety of sculptural and expressive architectural concepts emerged during the 1950s as a counter-movement to functionalism. The exiled Austrian architect, Friedrich Kiesler, worked on his biomorphic project, Endless House. In 1965, Bernard Rudofski published his book, "Architecture without Architects".

5

In 1949, Josef Frank wrote in a letter, "The ideals of [the pre-war period] are in fact no longer (nor should they be) those of the present and therefore they are also not good models. I think that all the veterans of the modern movement of that time think basically the same thing, but just keep muddling along, because they do not really know what one should do now, which I, by the way, also no longer know." And in another, later letter, he wrote that the worst aspect of post-war architecture was, "the loss of everything personal and everything following only a set pattern... Therefore, I believe that such buildings like the Seagram Building, the UNESCO in Paris (Breuer), etc, are so un-pleasant, because they all have even divisions without any three-dimensional or any other idea."

Double house, Weissenhofsiedlung Exhibition, Stuttgart, 1927

*Josef Frank and modernism*
Josef Frank, born in 1885 in the same year as Le Corbusier, was one of the pioneers and leaders of the modernist movement in Austria. Invited by Mies van der Rohe, Frank contributed a double house to the epoch-making Weissenhofsiedlung Exhibition in Stuttgart in 1927, he was Austria's representative at the first CIAM meeting in 1928, and designed and organised Vienna's Werkbundsiedlung in 1932. Frank designed workers' housing in Vienna at the

Interior and garden side, Villa Beer, Vienna, 1929-30

Villa Wehtje, Falsterbo, 1936

same time as he created villas and interior design schemes for wealthy clients in Austria and Sweden.

Josef Frank saw himself as a representative of the emergent modernist movement, but became, with time, increasingly critical of the way in which it developed. His criticism was primarily aimed at Germany and the Bauhaus school's all embracing design ideal, which developed into a new style that required conformance between buildings, interior, furniture and everyday goods.

Frank's criticism and success as an architect must be seen in combination with the softening of the strict modernism that occurred in the late 1920s and early 1930s, when the trend was towards softer and freer forms.

The starting point for Josef Frank in his own architecture was everyday things, little, personal things. He challenged "the boredom" through variation, and through the richness that arises when different aspects are brought together, free of demands for conformance. At the end of his text, "Das Haus als Weg und Platz" (The House as Path and Place) from 1931, Frank places modern architecture at the heart of the trivial and the everyday, in a string of simple questions: "... the rules governing what makes a building good do not change in principle, they must simply be seen in a new way. How do you enter the garden? What does the path to the entrance look like? How do you open the front door? What shape is the hall? How do you get from the hall, via the cloakroom, to the sitting room? How does the seating relate to doors and windows? There is no limit to the number of similar questions that must be answered, and it is of these elements that the house consists. This is modern architecture."

The central task of architecture, according to Frank, is the residential building. In addition to being "fit for purpose", Frank's houses and interiors include the purposeless in the form of movement, tranquillity, views, glimpses, openness, separation.

He rejects all forms of pathos in architecture but recognises man's need for kitsch and sentimentality in housing. Frank is drawn to the accidental, the unplanned and the intuitive. In his book "Architektur als Symbol" (1931) he writes, "Anyone today who wants to create something living must incorporate everything that currently lives. The entire Zeitgeist, including its sentimentality, its exaggerations, and its tastelessness, which are, at least, alive. […] Which is why the new art of building will be born out of our time's lack of good taste, out of the confusion, the variety and the sentimentality, out of everything living and which can be perceived: at last, the people's art, not art for the people."

8

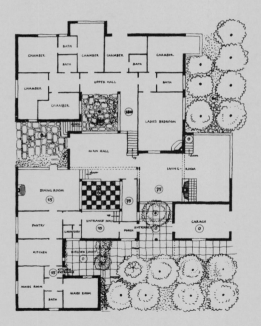

House for M. S., Los Angeles, project, 1930

Project for a house for Dagmar Grill in Skärgården, ca. 1926

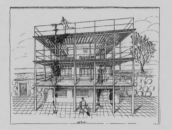

Project for a country house with three terraces, ca. 1926

Project for a country house with two terraces, ca. 1926

## Das Haus als Weg und Platz

Frank was involved in the reformulation of the way the room and space was seen that occurred in the early 1900s. In the 1800s, the room had been perceived as something static and closed. The room was equivalent to the interior, the inside of the house. But in the 1920s, this view was, in part, overturned. The modern room and space became synonymous with transparency. The room expanded to the outside of the house, it was no longer static, it was open and filled with light and air. For many modernist architects, the room was also something universal.

Frank was, through his architecture, deeply concerned with these space-related issues. In his own villa projects from the 1920s and 30s, he combines the modern dynamic room with an almost 19th century organisation in the layout. In his text, "Das Haus als Weg und Platz", Frank describes how one should move in a house as if through a town; narrow alleyways flow into open spaces that lead on to new passageways.

In the houses Frank designed in the 1920s and 30s, there is a constant and conscious shaping of movement through the houses; in the Villa Claëson in Falsterbo, it takes the form of a spiral movement up through the house, whilst in the Villa Wehtje, it is a well-directed sequence of rooms

9

that alternate between high and low, narrow and expansive. In a series of sketches for single-floor villas in Los Angeles, Frank develops the relationship between inside and outside through atrium courtyards. The outside is present far into the body of the house through the various courtyards of varying sizes.

One of Frank's most refined and spatially most composed housing projects from the 1920s, the Villa Wien XIII (1926), has a section where the beams have been displaced in relation to one another and the central section of the volume unit comprises a diagonal outdoor courtyard around which the rooms and the mass of the house are grouped.

## Back in Sweden

By 1933, Josef Frank and his Swedish wife had emigrated to Sweden, where in Stockholm, he became associated with the interior design firm, Svenskt Tenn.

In 1946, Frank returned to Stockholm after his war-time exile in New York. He carried out numerous interior design commissions for Svenskt Tenn, but the last house he had built was the Villa Wehtje in Falsterbo in 1936.

Frank spent much of the year abroad and maintained international contacts with certain old friends and colleagues, but in Stockholm, he was a peripheral figure in

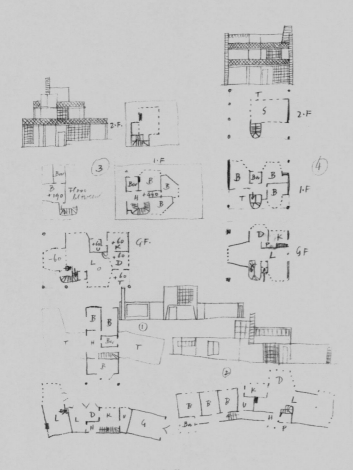

13 fantasy houses for Dagmar Grill, 1947

architectural circles. He held lectures occasionally and wrote the odd article.

Frank's isolation also affected the way he worked; from having been a key personality on the cultural scene in a major city, he was now an outsider. "I live pretty much alone here. I am, so to speak, stuck with myself and don't get out much, and then I start repeating myself."

Frank's exile also seems to have affected his attitude and willingness to plan houses. In a letter from 1946, he writes, "As you know, such tasks truly scare me: I would love to want to start building something new, but I have no idea how."

## 13 houses for Dagmar Grill

The 13 "letter houses" came about as a result of the encouragement given to Frank by his lady friend Dagmar Grill, that he once again involve himself in architectural projects. The sketches are an attempt to position himself before making a new start. The touchstone for Frank in these sketches is "complex" as a positive counter to the "boring" simplified mass production of post-war architecture. These houses, which were never built and which might not even have been intended for actual construction, may possibly mark the culmination of Josef Frank's work as an architect.

The 13 letters, dated 22nd July to 15th August 1947, contain sketches for 13 houses, and Frank's comments on them. In the 13 sketches, Frank develops concepts and ideas that he had tried in his Falsterbo villas and projects in Vienna, but he also experiments with completely new approaches. He investigates and develops movement through the houses, he articulates space with the aid of massive window openings and sealed sections. He experiments with the form of the buildings' volume units. Many of the projects also display a studied nonchalance in relation to the technical structure. Some of the projects introduce odd, completely disconnected elements. He stretches and plays with the boundaries of modernism in terms of choice of material, and introduces rural elements, such as the stone-clad chimneys against the white facades. The starting point for some of the projects is Le Corbusier's Domino system and free layout solutions, but they are married with Adolf Loos' Raumplan in one and the same project through the displacement of beams.

The projects display a remarkably composite nature, combining high and low. The fantasy houses are an attempt to redefine the boundaries of modernism, which had become too restrictive.

12

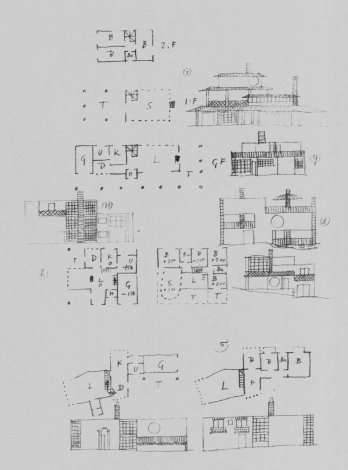

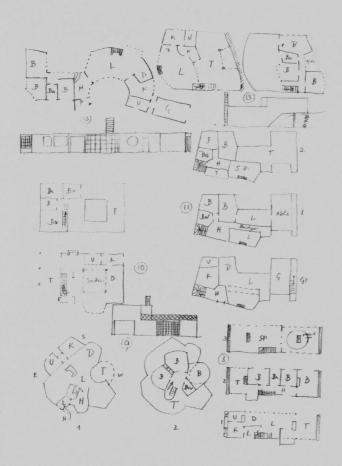

The most refined of the 13 house sketches – and the project that most satisfied Frank himself – is house 9. He has abandoned the rectangular and right-angled approach, creating instead completely irregular layouts. As early as 1931, he wrote, "The right-angled room is the type of room least suited to living in. It is very practical for storing furniture in, but not for anything else. I think that if one were to draw a random polygon with right angles or with obtuse ones, it would be a far more appropriate room layout than any regular right-angled shape. In the top-floor studio apartments, the random irregularities were a great help and they almost always make for a congenial and somewhat impersonal atmosphere."

In the letter to Dagmar Grill that accompanies fantasy house 9, Frank refers to the above text and once again says, "If you were to draw an irregular shape without reflecting on how it would look as a layout solution, wouldn't this still be a better solution than any carefully planned right-angled layout produced by some functionalist architect?"

## D-Houses and Double D-Houses

In December 1953, Frank drew a new series of 4 houses, which he called D-Houses, for Dagmar Grill. The four houses have similar programmatic structures – a large lounge and kitchen on the ground floor; one floor up, there are two bedrooms and a bathroom – which may suggest that Grill intended to build an actual house.

Frank was deliberately searching for a design language that was fully able to express and articulate his conviction that modern architecture must relate to every aspect of modern life; not just the pleasing and the beautiful, but the tensions and contradictions as well. In his houses from the 1920s and 30s, Frank had worked with the façade as a protective, unifying screen between outside and inside. With the 13 "letter houses" and, in D-House 2 in particular, he allows a variety of irregular shapes in the interior to be visible on the outside as well.

Frank's desire to give expression to everything that life has to offer, from the serious to the frivolous, is also apparent in another series of 6 houses that he designed for Grill, known as the Double D-Houses. They are all double houses, with one part intended for Grill and one intended for renting out. None of the plans are dated, but Frank designed these double houses before 1958. The designs of the two sections of the house differ. The one intended for Grill features greater variation and complexity in terms of room design, whilst the one intended for renting out is more conventionally designed. Several

House 9, 1947

Double D-House 4, mid 1950s

14

of these buildings display outright kitsch elements. "Every great work of art must border on kitsch," wrote Frank in an unpublished manuscript. "If people are so charmed by kitsch, then that at least is a genuine sentiment; they are not putting on airs. The work of art must speak to this legitimate feeling and shape it into a meaningful form."

## Accidentism

In a letter from the mid 1940s, written shortly after Frank returned to Stockholm after the war, he wrote, "I am now preoccupied here with the problem of boredom in art and architecture. Why, one must ask oneself, are the streets and dwellings here so uninteresting?" Frank compares the well-structured monotony of the European cities with New York's rich vitality, and asks himself if the American model is not a better one for the modern age. "I genuinely prefer the rawness there [in America]. I very much miss the whole Dyckman Street. What good is the art here and carefulness in building if everything is so dull? I am now completely of the opinion that much that is good comes about merely through chance and not through careful planning." Frank developed these thoughts on randomness

D-House 3rd december, 1953

in a text entitled "Accidentism", published in Form in 1958. The text is a sharp criticism of modernism and an attempt in part, to argue on behalf of his intentions in the houses he designed for Dagmar Grill.

At the heart of the text, he writes, "Every place where one feels comfortable – rooms, streets, and cities – has originated by chance."

The starting point for Accidentism comes from town planning – the most important architectural task, according to Frank – with its anonymous architecture without aesthetic correctness, with the pre-industrial cities that have evolved over a long period of time and their obvious irregular connections. "Accidentism […] consists in avoiding set forms and in making everything appear as if it had accidentally come about. This was more or less the case during older times […] Of course, one cannot leave everything to chance, it has to be orderly planned, but without rigorous order which is now overemphasised," writes Frank in a comment on his Accidentism text.

What Frank is proposing with Accidentism is not arbitrariness or giving chance a free hand; rather it is creating "as if it had occurred by chance". Frank's various imaginary house projects were just as controlled as any of his previous work. The differences and seemingly accidental composition of different sections of the projects are, in actual fact, the result of careful manipulation and control.

Frank never rejected modernism completely. His fundamental values from the 1920s are still present in his Accidentism concept, as he, himself, mentions. "I do not believe at all that one can build without principles, and I see no reason why one should deviate from the originally modern ones."

Abstractions and generalisations in architecture, as in other areas, are always exclusive in some respect: aesthetic and rational choices determine what will be included and what is inappropriate. Frank's thoughts on randomness are an attempt not to value different criteria, but rather, to provide scope for both high *and* low, good *and* bad taste. He strives to move away from an autonomous architecture towards the emotional, the everyday and the diverse, and at last – in his fantasy house projects – he arrives at a new "inclusive" architecture.

When it seems as though Frank has abandoned every theory and left everything to chance, it is, in actual fact, an attempt to avoid the fancies and whims of the planners, creating instead a truer and more correct relationship between architecture and real life.

Josef Frank (1885–1967)

# ACCIDENTISM
*Josef Frank*

The principles of shape in art have only been preserved through tradition; their validity cannot be proven. There is therefore no such thing as art without traditions. Since these rules have been observed everywhere from the most ancient times right up to our own day, one may regard them as "axiomatic". It is no easy task to assimilate traditions; if they do not belong to you, you cannot think freely within their framework and vary or expand the rules associated with them.

In our age of scientific thinking, all traditions are gradually being lost. There is no longer any reason to recognise laws that cannot be proven. Art and beauty have thus become dubious concepts that cannot be defined. If one does not have a tradition, one is forced to invent one's own artistic laws, which will then be relatively arbitrary. One also has to provide them with a moral or utilitarian, scientific or mystical motivation in order to be able to believe in them and spread this faith to others.

Such rules must therefore be extremely unambiguous and strict and allow no scope for deviations. The moral principles on which they rest are those of Puritanism, which appears to be the only accepted morality in this modern day and age, even if very few people actually abide by its fundamental principles. These artistic rules are therefore more negative than positive – much is forbidden but not much is allowed. If one wishes these days to acknowledge the superior aesthetic qualities of an object, it is generally done by using words such as "strict, sober, Spartan", whilst people distinguished by the qualities referred to by such epithets (particularly the last one) are by no means considered appealing.

We therefore now have art that not only bears little relation to our general modern view of life, but also symbolises its direct opposite. Whilst we hope that the art of tomorrow will be the kind of art that as many people as possible can have access to, today's art is increasingly insulating itself inside its own shell and appears to regard itself as something of an anachronism. Science lends its support for this belief in science, since science no longer tolerates any illusions that might impede its progress. Because of the exact sciences' connection with business, these sciences are sufficiently strong to hasten the demise of art.

Architecture, which may only in truly rare cases be called art, has abandoned this dangerous field and has thus been able to adapt to the new ideas. Its current forms of expression are conditioned by utilitarianism, and the other formative arts are now trying to follow the example set by architecture, even using its new materials to keep abreast of both development and business. And that is by no means all! All industrial products now tend to be included in the concept of art (a concept that has already been undermined and weakened), merging with it to form a single unit. This is taking place at a time when industry and art are more widely separated than ever before, while the means of production, which once were human hands, have now been altered beyond recognition.

The so-called designer, who thinks individualistically and thus is incapable of creating self-evident and typical forms, serves here as a mediator. His task is constantly to come up with innovations. While these innovations do possess a certain aesthetic value for a short period of time, they soon lose this value, giving way to new needs and encouraging the beauty-thirsting public to buy new things; the designer thus becomes a decorator. These activities transform everything into fashion items, which in turn influence the art created in its surrounding environment. Fashion sensations are, as we know, extremely seductive, as they can relieve the monotony inherent in the standardisation necessitated by mass production.

The activities of such fashion designers consist mainly of altering functional forms and – where this is not possible – of disguising and decorating them. The archetypal example is the most popular technical product of our age, the motorcar, whose shape now exercises an influence on all human creations. Both horse-drawn vehicles and steam engines were designed autonomously by their originators and therefore possessed the natural beauty of the self-evident. The motorcar's bodywork, on the other hand, is a relatively arbitrary composition, and its shape is not determined by practical considerations alone. It changes for no apparent reason according to the fashion of the day. All objects produced in this way always have something unoriginal about them; they deviate from their natural shape. And this is precisely what the public finds beautiful; take our modern cutlery, for example. The exaltation of good taste involves sacrificing character, and the levelling tendency inherent in this is inimical to art. Our most urgent need today is not uniformity, but as clear a distinction as possible between utility goods and works of art. A work of art is an end in itself and cannot be used to produce something else or to serve a specific purpose.

Our living space should therefore not be regarded as a work of art; nowadays, anyone who designs such a living space, or has it designed by an artist, will almost always try to give it precisely the kind of unchanging harmony that will make it into a work of art. To stimulate him, he will find a multitude of models in the pages of magazines and at exhibitions, which, for propaganda reasons, must of course always have an element of theatrical decoration. With the help of stylish objects and colour harmonies, attempts are made to create something that the room's occupant will consider beautiful and therefore regard as art; he will even select paintings that are suited to the room's colour scheme, for which purpose he will imagine himself to have a favourite colour. What he is looking for is an effective backdrop, nothing more. A sitting room in which one can live and think freely is neither beautiful, nor harmonious, nor photogenic. It is the result of a series of random accidents; it is never really completed and it has sufficient scope to include whatever may be needed to satisfy its owner's shifting requirements.

I use the example of a sitting room here because I wish to arrive at an architectural principle; the sitting room is, for us, the ultimate goal of architecture, so to speak, it is the architectural component that is closest to us. I therefore find it more appropriate to use this changeable space as a starting point and then build on it, rather than going in the opposite direction by regarding the sitting room as a kind of consequence of some specific architectural style and try to adapt it to suit this style.

The prerequisites for making a living space comfortable also apply to houses, streets and cities, whose current inelegant design renders their inhabitants homeless. This inelegance is not governed by necessity; it rests essentially on aesthetic preconceptions. What we need is a much higher degree of elasticity, not stringent principles of shape; what we need is a demonumentalisation, without lapsing into historic styles. These styles are now and will continue to be dead. What I term modern architecture (not just the architecture that was modern during the first half of 1958) differs in principle from all historic styles of architecture. The essence of a style consists in its use of plastic forms, such as capitals, mouldings, etc., which clarify the building's static dimension to the eye. The creation of harmony between construction components that are either bearing or borne used to be considered the prime task of architecture. These symbols were crucial to their day; without them, it was impossible to feel safe. We, however, no longer have any use for them; we think in scientific terms and therefore rely on structural calculations, even if we do not understand them. With the loss of these static symbols, the participation of the sculptor in architecture, formerly an essential and organic component, is also lost. Architecture has now been thrown back on its own devices, the grouping of construction elements. Only through this grouping can one achieve the plasticity that is so crucial to the overall appearance of the city and its shifting expressions of life. This does not mean that I consider all plastic decoration on buildings an impossibility. What I do mean is that it is no longer an organic component; it is something that is added on and that cannot characterise the building itself, although, in some cases, it is desirable in order to relieve the monotony.

The three formative arts, however, are today separated from each other; since the co-operation that existed in the age of historic styles is no longer possible, each of these arts is free to choose its own path. It was often the plastic details of a building, the work of a sculptor that was mainly found on its façades, which turned works of architecture into works of art. It is no longer possible for us to use such additions to transform any particular type of building, originally designed to be useful, into something approaching a work of art. Architecture can now only reach the level of art when the function of a building is extremely simple in comparison with the significance of its form, for example in the case of a church. Its practical requirements involve nothing but the creation of a space that may, in principle, take any shape; in this context, we must also admit that any Gothic church fills its function better than a modern one. But here all such complete freedom is possible, something that otherwise can only be achieved in provisional exhibition pavilions, and even these, as we know, have had an influence on architecture.

The progression of the various styles has always been the same. Initially, all is strict and simple within the framework of rigid laws that soon become monotonous and dull. Hence, people start to demand variety, and since no changes in terms of principle are required, such variety is achieved by enriching the forms with the help of decorations and playful constructions. These eventually become so extreme that the value of the original principles can be called into question, resulting in a return to a new form of simplicity that will symbolise the ideas of a new age.

New styles appear not for practical reasons but to accompany the emergence of a new ideology. A style can be defined as the visible expression of the symbols of an epoch, or as the symbol of a faith which, once it ceases to exist, is seen as superstition. In the age of historic styles, the various formative arts used many of the same symbols, thus giving rise to universal styles. As scientific thinking progressed, these have gradually disappeared. What we have gained thereby is the chance to provide every object with its own functional and characteristic form. This has given us freedom, as well as a diversity hitherto neither necessary nor required. People, however, are ill at ease with this freedom, which is why there is no shortage these days of examples of the revival of various superstitions. We have thus started to yearn once again for a universal style that will reflect a harmonious universe, the fundamental principle of all mysticism. A harmony in which monuments and machines are dissimilar can no longer be imagined. Modern architecture had only just made its breakthrough when the other formative arts – for no obvious reason – began to adapt to its forms to achieve the desired uniformity. Even utility goods had to adapt. This was achieved with the help of expressionless geometric forms that displaced the organic ones. Thus began, on mystical grounds in the midst of all the objectivity, our decorative age in which fashion trends affect everything around us.

Modern architecture cannot thank practicality for its popular success. Any modern building might just as easily have been erected in one of the historic styles with no detriment to its usefulness. The new aesthetic effects associated with the symbols of our age can be achieved with the help of new materials and constructions, and they are the persuasive element. Modern architecture also has its own symbols, but these are no longer static. I will mention only one of the most important, the flat roof, whose practical advantages are by no means so significant that they alone could have given rise to such impassioned discussions. It can, however, be used as a symbol for logical thinking, sealing off the upper regions at the top of the house and preventing the creation of the attic, an ambiguous and irrational space full of mystery.

One cannot really imagine a dialogue such as the following one (taken from Ibsen's "The Wild Duck") taking place in a modern house:

HEDVIG: …whenever I happen to remember everything in there… then it always seems as if that whole room… ought to be called "the ocean's depths"… (and) it's only an attic.

GREGER: Are you so sure of that?

HEDVIG: That it's an attic?

GREGER: Yes. Do you know that for certain?

We now long once again if not exactly for attics, at least for rooms that allow scope for the imagination, rather than simply rooms that contain separate sections for the apartment's various functions, such as eating and sleeping, et cetera. We long for streets that are something other than simply traffic problems, however neatly solved they may be.

Just as the symbols of all historic styles could symbolise something other than the static context, so can the shapes of modern architecture. In 1851, Semper wrote: "What a great injustice is not done to us architects when we are accused of lacking inventiveness, because a new, forcefully and emphatically implemented idea of historical and global proportions is nowhere to be found. Come up with a new idea first, and then we will surely find the appropriate architectonic expression for it."

By "expression", Semper meant the symbols of a new society. In the last decades, we have seen more than enough examples of new societies. Not one of them, however, has been capable of producing anything resembling its own art. They were all free to select what they wished from what was in front of them, adapting what they chose to fit in with their own tendencies. The trends were only determined by force and it is thus extremely debatable whether they really are symbols of the societies that use them, even in our so-called free Western world.

Here too, it is difficult to liberate oneself from totalitarian symbols. Stimulated by the association with industry and its standardisation, modern architecture began to adopt the same tendencies towards uniformity, unsuspecting of what this involved. At that time, there were even heretics' tribunals that dictated what was and was not permitted. A standardisation process that goes over and above what is useful and becomes an aesthetic ideal is barbaric, and encourages the uniforming of people affected by such an environment. Today it would hardly seem that the idea of free thinking is an "idea that has been implemented forcefully and emphatically". Artists, however, are prophets; any attempt to propagate this idea would be welcome, just as the artists of their day with such persistent success advocated subsequent totalities. One of the consequences of this propaganda being the monotonous character of our cities.

Every human being needs a certain amount of sentiment in order to feel comfortable; people are deprived of this when they are forced to impose moral demands on everything. What people need is variety, not stereotypical monumentalism. Nobody feels comfortable in an ordered environment that is forced on them, however well disguised it might be by the touch of beauty. What I therefore have to propose is not so much new rules and forms as a completely new approach to art. Away with universal styles, away with all standardisation of industry and art, away with the whole complex of ideas that has gained popularity under the name of functionalism! I propose replacing this system of architecture with a new one. As is the practice these days, I propose to give it a name that explains its main tendency: for the time being, I will call it "accidentism" to make it clear that we should be creating an environment that appears to have arisen by accident.

All places in which we feel comfortable – rooms, streets and cities – have arisen by accident; in cities that grow organically, buildings from all epochs stand side by side in harmony. And while we cannot achieve this today,

I am convinced that our uniformity has not arisen for practical reasons but as a result of an ideology – an ideology that is not even our own. The older symbols of architecture, which once offered variety, no longer exist. We now need far stronger means and larger dimensions in order to achieve plastic effects. The aesthetic value of individual houses is no longer of such great significance, even if we have no wish to underestimate it. What we see on a street is shop-fronts and silhouettes. This is why urban planning is architecture's most important problem. What variety offers us is character rather than generalised beauty. A theatre does not have to look like a factory, any more than a bank has to resemble a bakery.

The idea of "elevating" everything to the level of art is of course highly seductive. But let us not forget one thing: even if we cannot define what a work of art is, one of its essential attributes is that it is unchanging and serves no purpose other than to be looked at. In this sense, it imposes demands on people, and I do not believe that one can, in the long run, feel completely comfortable in an environment consisting only of objects that impose such demands.

*Originally published in Swedish in* FORM, *1958*

## 13 FANTASY HOUSES FOR DAGMAR GRILL

## HOUSE 1

*The earliest of these fantasy houses appear in a series of letters written by Josef Frank in 1947 and addressed to his wife's cousin, Dagmar Grill. Frank had known her since the first decade of the 20th century, when she lived and worked in Vienna. Following the death of Frank's wife in 1957, she and Frank lived together in Stockholm. At the time, Frank had no construction projects to work on and Dagmar Grill therefore encouraged him to make the sketches. All these houses feature more or less the same room layout.*

*The 13 letters, dated between 22nd July and 15th August 1947, contain sketches of 13 houses, along with Frank's own comments on them. Some time later, Frank collected the sketches on three sheets of drawing paper (p11-13). He numbered them 1-13, and over the next few years, he produced a number of watercolours and continued to develop the plans for the projects. Frank also altered the chronological order of the collection. Originally, it was as follows: 1, 2, 5, 6, 7, 4, 3, 9, 8, 10, 11, 12, 13.*

This is a later version of the sketch contained in a letter dated 22nd July 1947. Frank referred to it as "The New Dybelhouse No 1".

It is distinguished by its rectangular body placed at right angles over an elongated less regularly shaped structure. The ground floor houses the sitting room, eating area, garage and storage space. The protruding sections of the upper structure rest on special supports and house the bedrooms. Beneath these protruding sections, Frank has created an outdoor anteroom in front of the entrance, as well as a patio area adjoining the sitting room. The long narrow sitting room ends in an open fireplace and a large bay window, easily recognisable from Frank's earlier projects. The stairway leading to the upper floor is laterally placed on one side of the entrance.

A partially erased rail has been sketched on the roof of the north wing, indicating that Frank had planned a rooftop terrace here. The façades of the house are completely smooth, while the chimney structures are built of contrasting brickwork.

House 1, model

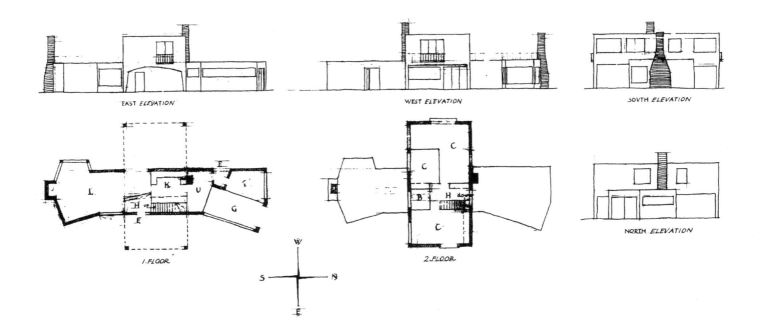

EAST ELEVATION

WEST ELEVATION

SOUTH ELEVATION

1.FLOOR

2.FLOOR

NORTH ELEVATION

House I, 1947, elevations, plans

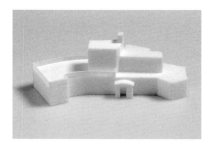

House 2, model

## HOUSE 2

Frank referred to this later version of the sketch contained in his letter dated 23rd July 1947 as "Dybelhouse No 2".

Once again, this is an elongated single-storey house, with an irregular and apparently arbitrary free layout with a glazed studio built on the roof. Frank refers to this as a "complex house on the roof", and it is reached by a stairway ascending from the hallway. This stairway also divides the sitting room area from the dining room and fireplace area. The bedroom area is located separately a few steps up from the entrance, as in most of Frank's single-storey houses.

The exterior of the house is distinguished by Frank's skilful and playful use of mullioned/transom windows alternating with picture windows, emphasising the complexity of the house. This complexity is achieved by using a series of structural volumes at different levels.

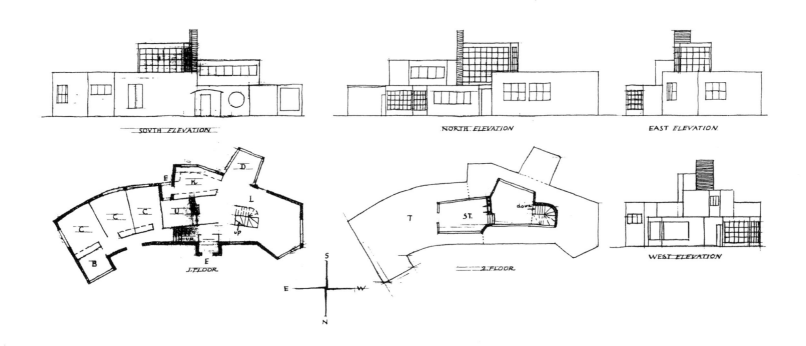

SOUTH ELEVATION

NORTH ELEVATION

EAST ELEVATION

WEST ELEVATION

J. FLOOR

2. FLOOR

House 2, 1947, elevations, plans

29

## HOUSE 5

Frank referred to this later version of the sketch contained in a letter dated 25th July 1947 as "The New Dybelhouse".

This elongated two-storey house makes a unified impression in terms of its structural volume, since the base of the roof remains at the same height throughout the structure. Only the entrance stands out in that it is lower than the rest of the house. A rectangular area houses the bedrooms, garage and kitchen and is combined with a less regular-shaped sitting room that is twice as high as the other rooms. The sitting room is located a few steps above the eating area, and the open stairway then proceeds to the upper storey. Both the upper hallway and the eating area on the ground floor open onto the sitting room. The irregularly shaped terrace on the upper level is subordinated to the main body of the house, and its curved wall cuts into the upper part of the sitting room, bringing an exciting variation to the room and forming a more intimate section underneath. The sitting room is reached via the entrance hall.

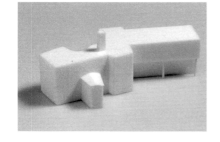

House 5, model

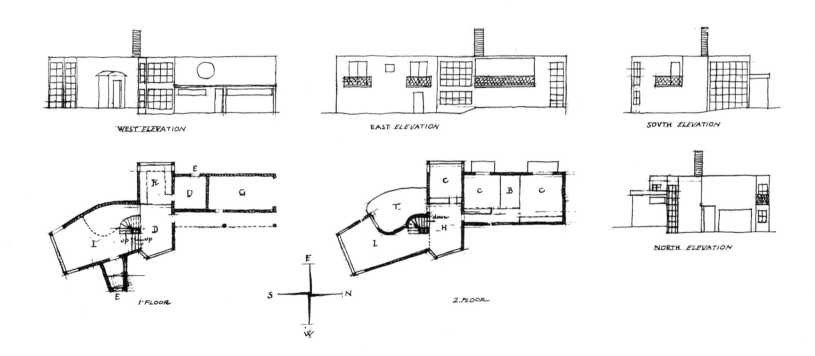

WEST ELEVATION

EAST ELEVATION

SOVTH ELEVATION

NORTH ELEVATION

1·FLOOR

2·FLOOR

House 5, 1947, elevations, plans

## HOUSE 6

This is a later version of the sketch contained in a letter dated 29th July 1947.

The layout of the house presented in this proposal features a more or less square-shaped floor plan on two levels. The communal sections of the house feature irregular shapes both on the ground floor and in the glazed rooftop studio. Frank's comments on his sketch: "Things are now getting increasingly complex" The house has great spatial complexity, with its central section on two levels connecting the studio above with the sitting room and eating area on the ground floor. The open stairway in the sitting room leads to a bedroom area on the first landing and another on the same level as the studio. The outer body of the house falls back to the west and its terraces face south and west.

House 6, model

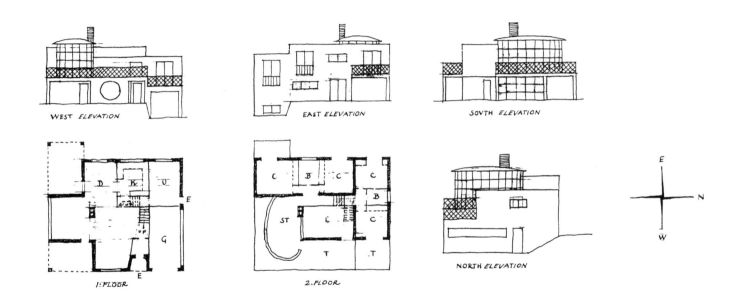

WEST *ELEVATION*

EAST *ELEVATION*

SOVTH *ELEVATION*

NORTH *ELEVATION*

1: FLOOR

2. FLOOR

House 6, 1947, elevations, plans

33

## HOUSE 7

This is a later version of the sketch contained in a letter dated 30th July 1947.

House 7, the fifth in the sequence, is altogether new and different. It includes several gently sloping roofs, and both the pillars supporting the roofs and the beams used in the joist systems of the various levels are placed more or less at random. In the letter that refers to this project, Frank comments: "with a roof, but complex." Inside, the house's communal area is located on the ground floor, and there is a magnificent covered terrace one floor up. The house's bedrooms are reached via the central stairway.

House 7, model

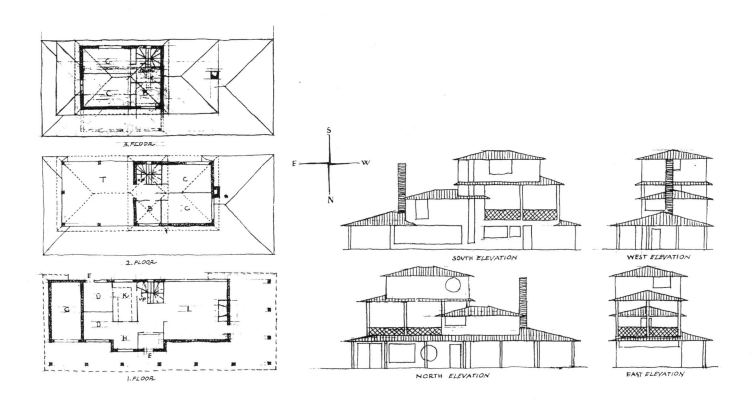

3. FLOOR

2. FLOOR

1. FLOOR

S
E — W
N

SOUTH ELEVATION

WEST ELEVATION

NORTH ELEVATION

EAST ELEVATION

House 7, 1947, elevations, plans

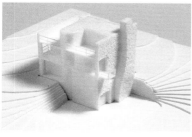

House 4, model

## HOUSE 4

This is a later version of the sketch contained in a letter dated 31st July 1947.

This house, number 6 in the series, is one of Frank's more compact structures. It is based on a rectangular grid of squares where each storey develops freely within the framework of the natural stone walls of the gables. The edges of the beams can be detected on the two lengths of the house in the form of horizontally highlighted rails that contrast strangely with the rough-hewn and rural stonework of the gables. The plan was for a three-storey, semi-subterranean house, with basement, studio and rooftop terrace.

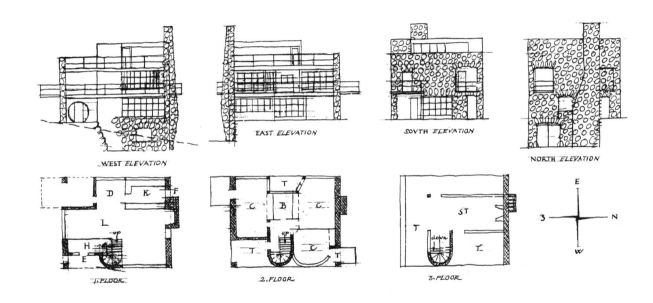

WEST *ELEVATION* EAST *ELEVATION* SOVTH *ELEVATION* NORTH *ELEVATION*

1.FLOOR 2.FLOOR 3.FLOOR

House 4, 1947, elevations, plans

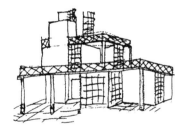

## HOUSE 3

This is a later version of the sketch contained in a letter dated 1st August 1947 and is the seventh in the series.

Once again, this house is based on a rectangular grid of squares within which each storey lives its own life.

As in House 4, Frank uses Le Corbusier's "Domino System" and "Plan Libre" as his starting point. The plan is modified in the letter's sketch by applying Loos' "Raumplan" principle where different levels house different rooms. Frank abandons this principle completely in his later version. The various levels of beams and terraces do not coincide with the different storeys. Frank refers to the house as being in the "Chinese style".

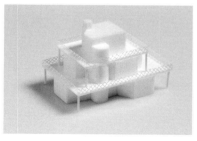

House 3. model

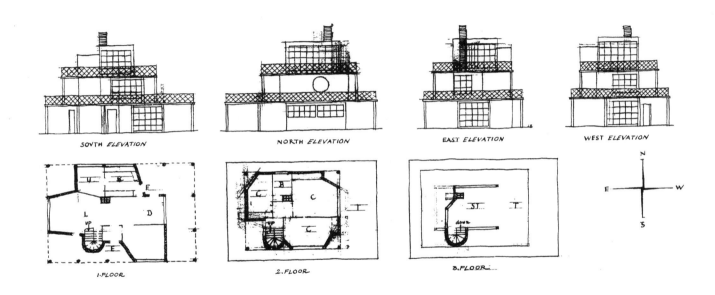

SOVTH *ELEVATION*   NORTH *ELEVATION*   EAST *ELEVATION*   WEST *ELEVATION*

1·FLOOR   2.FLOOR   3.FLOOR

House 3, 1947, elevations, plans

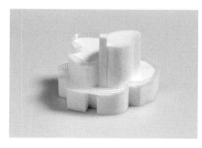

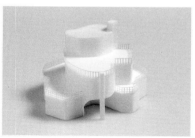

House 9, model

## HOUSE 9

This is a later version of the sketch contained in a letter dated 4th August 1947.

This project was sketched 3 days after the sketch of House 3 was made, and Frank has now totally abandoned rectangular shapes and right angles, creating two separate irregularly shaped layouts. As early as 1931, in the text of "Das Haus als Weg und Platz", Frank wrote the following: "The right-angled room is the type of room least suited to living in. It is very practical for storing furniture in, but not for anything else. I think that if one were to draw a random polygon with right angles or with obtuse ones, it would be a far more appropriate room layout than any regular right-angled shape. In the top-floor studio apartments, the random irregularities were a great help and they almost always make for a congenial and somewhat impersonal atmosphere."

In the letter to Dagmar Grill that accompanies the sketch of the plans for House 9, Frank refers to the article above: "If you were to draw an irregular shape without reflecting on how it would look as a layout solution, wouldn't this still be a better solution than any carefully planned right-angled layout produced by some functionalist architect?"

House 9 is the one that Frank was most pleased with, and later he refers to it as the "Accidental House". His plan is drawn on a scale of 1:100 and he also produced a watercolour of the project to illustrate his "Accidentism" article, which appeared over 10 years later. In the caption, the article refers to the project as the "House for Djursholm", stating that the outline of the house was drawn without taking its contents into consideration.

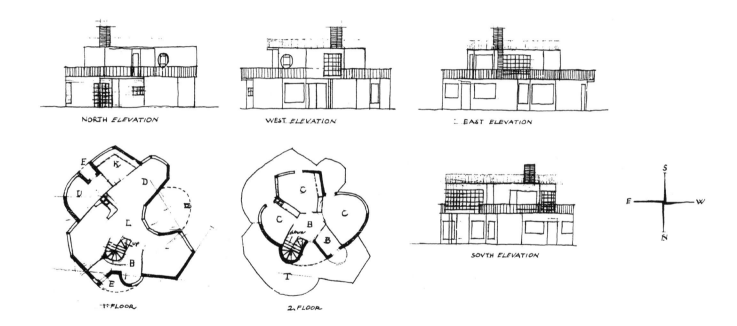

NORTH *ELEVATION*

WEST *ELEVATION*

*EAST ELEVATION*

SOVTH *ELEVATION*

1ᵗᵗ *FLOOR*

2. *FLOOR*

House 9, 1947, elevations, plans

House 9, watercolour

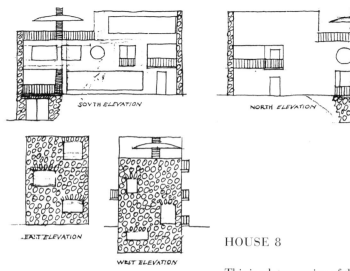

SOUTH ELEVATION

NORTH ELEVATION

EAST ELEVATION

WEST ELEVATION

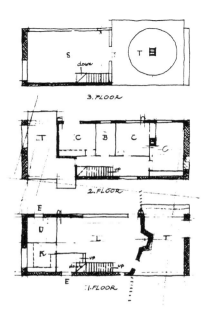

3. FLOOR

2. FLOOR

1. FLOOR

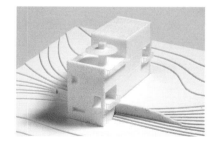

House 8, model

# HOUSE 8

This is a later version of the sketch contained in a letter dated 5th August 1947.

In this elongated house, Frank returns once more to the rectangular layout. The house is similar to House 4, but this time, Frank experiments by breaking up the main body of the house with the help of a number of terraces framed by stone walls. The holes in the façades are offset by the various window designs and sizes. The materials used include stone, plaster and concrete. In his letter to Grill, Frank writes: "The house is not very complex, just slightly. We can vary it later on."

House 8, 1947, elevations, plans

House 8, watercolour

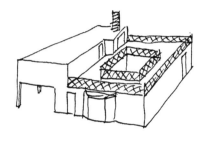

## HOUSE 10

This is a later version of the sketch contained in a letter dated 6th August 1947.

House 10 also follows a rectangular layout and the outside appears relatively sealed. The house features an open atrium in the middle of the main structure, allowing light to flow in and making for an open feeling. The sitting room, eating area and large bay window facing east are all grouped around the atrium. The upper storey houses bedrooms and leads out onto the rooftop terrace, which juts out above the front door and the south-facing terrace adjoining the sitting room. Frank comments: "It's not very complex – but it's very good, and one could always make it more complex." Here, Frank returns to the atrium courtyards that he used so often in projects from the 1920s and 1930s.

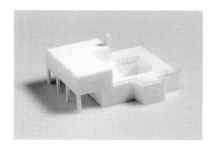

House 10, model

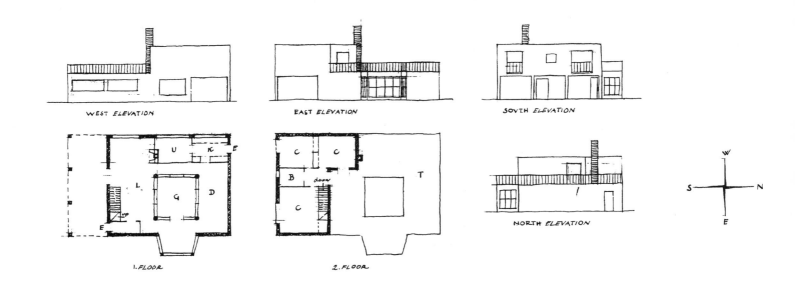

WEST ELEVATION

EAST ELEVATION

SOUTH ELEVATION

NORTH ELEVATION

1. FLOOR

2. FLOOR

House 10, 1947, elevations, plans

## HOUSE 11

This is a later version of the sketch contained in a letter dated 12th August 1947.

In the last three houses, numbered 11, 12 and 13, Frank once again abandons his strict right-angled layout. Just like House 9, these houses consist of completely irregular rooms that do not seem to follow any specific order, planned room sequence or hierarchy. House 11 is larger than the previous ones and consists of a right-angled, two-storey section with a studio and garage combined with an irregularly shaped three-storey body. The front door and hall with the laterally placed stairway up to the bedroom area are located on the ground floor, where the sitting room and dining area surround an open courtyard facing south. Frank's own comment to Dagmar Grill, is: "this is a large D-house, but it doesn't matter much, since on paper, it doesn't cost anything."

House 11, model

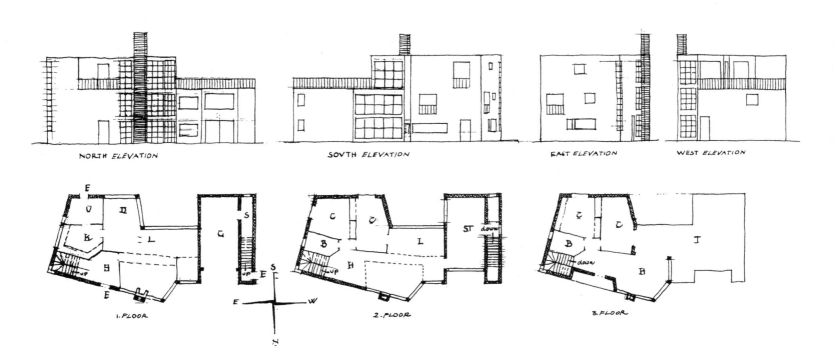

NORTH ELEVATION

SOVTH ELEVATION

EAST ELEVATION

WEST ELEVATION

1. FLOOR

2. FLOOR

3. FLOOR

House II, 1947, elevations, plans

## HOUSE 12

This is a later version of the sketch contained in the letter dated 14th August 1947

House 12 is a single-storey house that extends along an open, semi-circular, south-facing courtyard with an irregular curve and large windows giving onto the hallway and sitting room. The communal section of the house follows the curved shape, and the bay windows and chimney structures lend a specific rhythm and pattern to the outer wall opposite. The bedroom area is rectangular and is located a few steps up from the hallway. At the meeting point between the various sections of the house, there is an open, rectangular, north-facing court-yard. The layout of the house is reminiscent of the layout of Villa Wehtje.

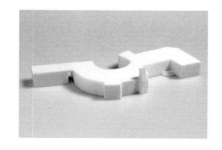

House 12, model

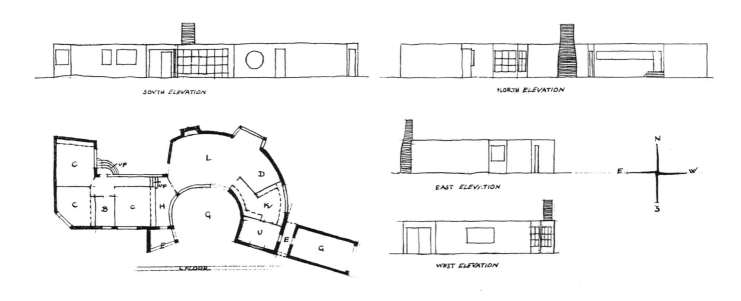

SOUTH ELEVATION

NORTH ELEVATION

EAST ELEVATION

WEST ELEVATION

House 12, 1947, elevation, plan

51

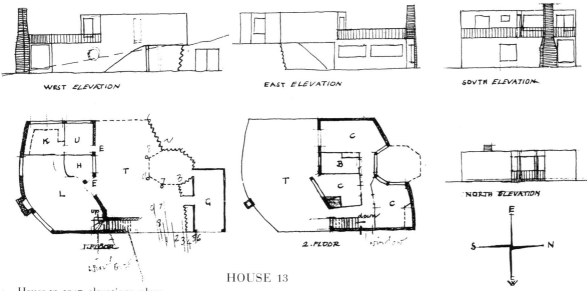

WEST ELEVATION  EAST ELEVATION  SOUTH ELEVATION

NORTH ELEVATION

1. FLOOR

2. FLOOR

HOUSE 13

House 13, 1947, elevations, plans

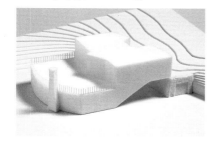

House 13, model

This is a later version of the sketch contained in a letter dated 15th August 1947.

The site is located on a slope that contributes to the step-like structure of the different storeys, and the entrance is reached via the covered courtyard below the structure. There is also a terrace outside the bedrooms on the upper storey. The irregularly shaped sitting room and eating area are located on the ground floor. The sketches were reworked by Frank on a scale of 1:100, as well as in a watercolour.

House 13, watercolour

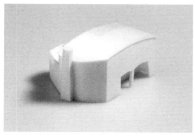

D-House 2nd December, model

## D-HOUSES

*Between 2nd – 9th December 1953, Frank drew a new series of 4 houses for Dagmar Grill, which he referred to as D-Houses. The four houses have similar layouts, with a large sitting room and kitchen on the bottom floor and two bedrooms and a bathroom one floor up. This may indicate that Grill was actually intending to build the house. None of the plans have regular rectangular shapes and most of the room shapes are irregular. There is no hint of differentiated ceiling heights between the various storeys. The first, third and fourth houses, all combine plain right-angled rooms with irregular ones in a manner that is reminiscent of Houses 4 and 13 from 1947.*

## D-HOUSE 2ND DECEMBER

This is one of the few projects in which Frank does not use a flat roof. The domed roof holds the main structure together and is reflected in the sitting room's freely curving wall. The stairway up to the bedroom level divides the large room into a dining area and sitting room and the house also features an arch motif.

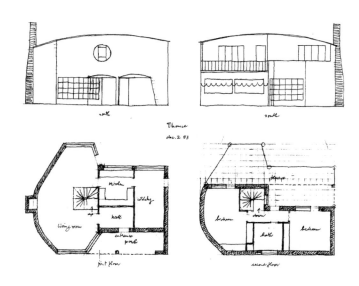

D-House 2nd December, elevations, plans

D-House 2nd December, watercolours

D-House 2nd December, watercolours

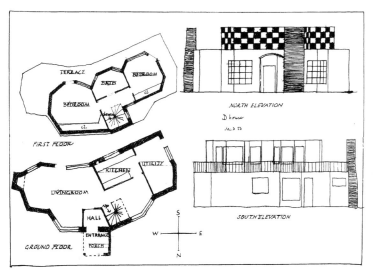

D-House 3rd December, elevations, plans

D-House 3rd December, model

# D-HOUSE 3RD DECEMBER

This is the second house in the sequence and is dated 3rd December. It is curiously complex, and Frank has added completely new elements, such as the chequered superstructure with its terraces on all sides. Even more than the 13 sketches in the letters, this sketch expresses a conscious ambivalence when it comes to the relationships between the various parts of the house. The façade is both simple and artful – a paradox that gives the house its underlying tension.

D-House 3rd December, watercolour

## D-HOUSE 5TH DECEMBER

This is the third house in the sequence and the only one with three storeys and rooftop terraces at different levels. The façade of the house has a sealed appearance on the entrance side, and only the front door is highlighted by its special structure and large round window. The courtyard side, however, is freer and more open and features many bay windows. The sitting room lies directly beyond the entrance hall and has two large bay windows and a fireplace at the back. A stairway in the hall leads up to the bedrooms.

D-House 5th December, model

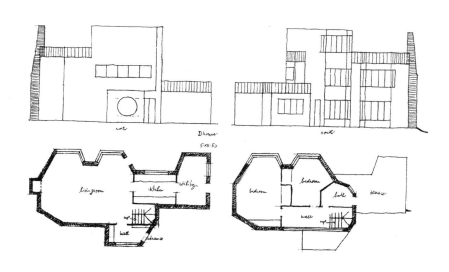

D-House 5th December, elevations

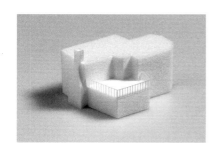

D-House 9th December, model

## D-HOUSE 9<sup>TH</sup> DECEMBER

Once again, this D-house has a level façade with a sealed appearance on the entrance side and two circular windows as its hallmark. The rear of the house is more varied and open, with terraces and lower structures. Once again, the stairway inside leading up to the bedrooms divides the large room into an eating area and sitting room.

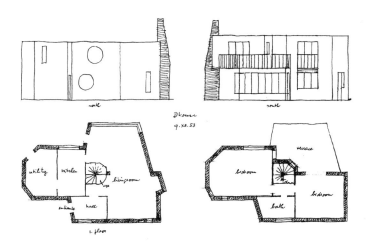

north

south

D-house
9.XII.53

utility   kitchen   livingroom

entrance   hall

1. floor

terrace

bedroom

bath   bedroom

D-House 9th December, elevations, plans

A D-house, model

## DOUBLE D-HOUSES

*Frank's desire to express all that life has to offer, from the sublime to the ridiculous, is also displayed in an additional series of 6 houses that he drew for Grill. They are all double houses with almost the same room layout. They all have one section intended for Grill herself, and another that she could rent out. There is no date on any of the drawings, although Frank probably drew these double houses during the period before 1958.*

*The design used for each of the two sections of the houses is different. The section intended for Grill displays more variation and spatial complexity, while the other section intended for renting is more conventional. The façades display a more individual design than in the previous series, with stairways, for example, placed in the façade. This is particularly true of the entrance side, while the rear of the house is less striking.*

## A D-HOUSE

This D-house adheres for the most part to a right-angled layout. The bottom floor of the section intended for Grill consists of a kitchen, a hallway and a large room divided by the stairway. This large room has several niches and bay windows, and it features spatial variations in terms of the height of the room, as well as views up to the upper storey. The entrance side features a series of downward steps, starting with the low-slung wind-shelter at the front door. The rear of the house is less striking, with elements similar to bay windows stretching from ground level to roof base. (The different storeys in the sketch have been incorrectly labelled).

A D-house, watercolour

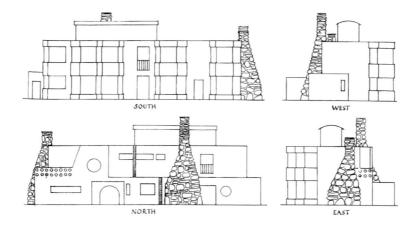

A D-house, elevations, plans

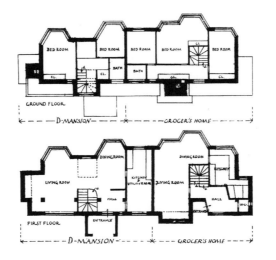

BED ROOM  BED ROOM  BED ROOM  BED ROOM  CL.  BED ROOM

BATH  CL.  BATH  CL.  CL.

CL.  BATH  BATH  CL.

GROUND FLOOR

← - - D·MANSION - - →  ← - - GROCER'S HOME - - →

DINING ROOM  DINING ROOM

KITCHEN  KITCHEN

LIVING ROOM  UTILITY ROOM  LIVING ROOM

HALL  HALL  W·C·

FIRST FLOOR  ENTRANCE  ENTRANCE

← - - - D·MANSION - - - →  ← - - - GROCER'S HOME - - - →

A D-HOUSE

S
E ✦ W
N

Another D-house, model

## ANOTHER D-HOUSE

The second D-house adheres for the most part to an elongated rectangular layout featuring room height variations.
The bottom floor houses the kitchen, the front door area, a
hallway and a dining area, with a few steps leading up to the
sitting room. The opening in front of the chimney wall
means that the sitting room is open right up to the level of
the upper hallway. The stairway is located in the sitting
room and forms a sculptural feature in the entrance façade
of both sections of the house. Grill's section of the rear of the
house is also more ornate in this plan.

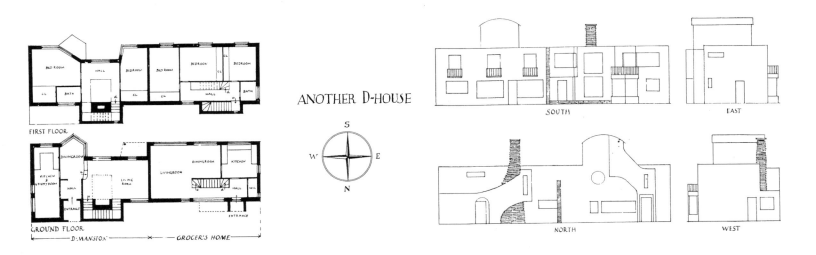

FIRST FLOOR

GROUND FLOOR
— D. MANSION — × — GROCER'S HOME —

ANOTHER D-HOUSE

SOUTH

EAST

NORTH

WEST

Another D-house, elevations, plans

69

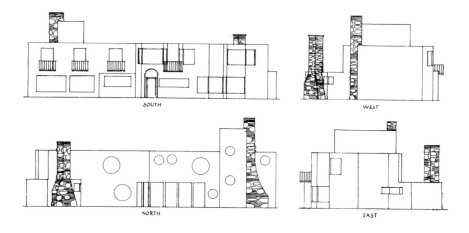

SOUTH     WEST

NORTH     EAST

THIRD D-HOUSE

S
E    W
N

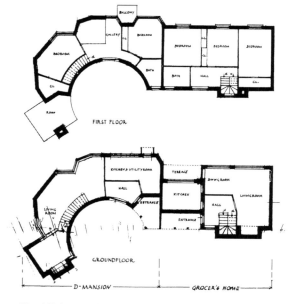

FIRST FLOOR

GROUNDFLOOR

D-MANSION     GROCER'S HOME

Third D-house, elevations, plan

## THIRD D-HOUSE

The third house introduces a rounded open courtyard in front of the entrance. The layout is reminiscent of House 12 in the sketches contained in the 1947 letters. The most striking feature of the house is the design of the front with its 9 round windows of varying sizes and its two stone-covered chimney structures. The plan itself is also interesting, with its elongated curved sitting room and different levels, as well as the open stairway leading up to the bedrooms.

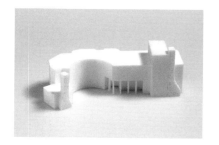

Third D-house, model

Third D-house, watercolour

FIRST FLOOR

GROUND FLOOR

D-MANSION        GROCER'S HOME

D-house 4, elevations, plans

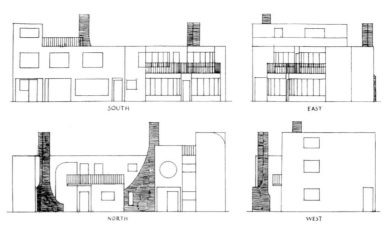

SOUTH

EAST

NORTH

WEST

## D-HOUSE 4

The fourth Double D-house is even more explicit in its gentle irony, with its pink plaster on the front of the house and its stone-covered chimney structures in the shape of two giraffes. Although the exterior displays Frank's playful side, the spatial sequence has been carefully planned. The exterior is a direct consequence of the interior layout. The house depicted in the watercolour displays elements of pure kitsch, recalling Frank's own statement in an unpublished manuscript: "Every great work of art must border on kitsch. If people are so charmed by kitsch, then that at least is a genuine sentiment: they are not putting on airs. The work of art must speak to this legitimate feeling and shape it into a meaningful form."

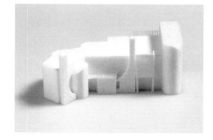

D-house 4, model

D-house 4, watercolour

73

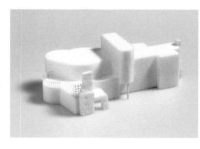

D-house 5. model

## D-HOUSE 5

D-house 5 is the next house in the series and its greater complexity stems from the fact that the different storeys are totally independent of each other and have completely different shapes in the section intended for Grill. There is no shifting of levels, although the upper storey does jut out, creating space for a terrace area off the sitting room below it. An imposing chimney structure featuring natural stone makes up one side of the upper terrace and gives it a fireplace, as well as being a feature of the house's front entrance. The irregularly shaped sitting room is screened from the eating area by the curved stairway leading to the upper floor. (The points of the compass specified in the drawing are not correct.)

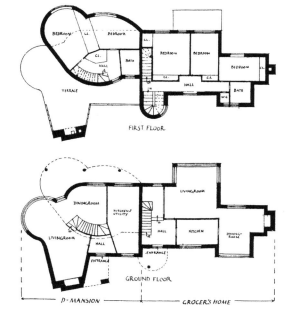

BEDROOM CL. BEDROOM
CL.
BATH CL. BEDROOM BEDROOM
HALL BATH CL. BEDROOM CL.
CL. HALL
TERRACE W·C BATH

FIRST FLOOR

DINING ROOM LIVING ROOM
KITCHEN & UTILITY
LIVING ROOM HALL KITCHEN DINING ROOM
HALL
ENTRANCE ENTRANCE

GROUND FLOOR

D-MANSION                    GROCER'S HOME

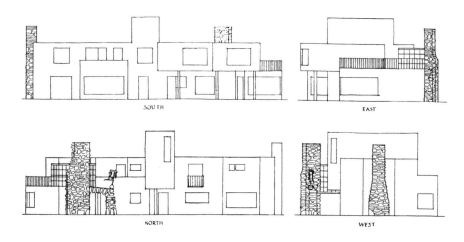

SOUTH                    EAST

NORTH                    WEST

# D·HOUSE 5

N
E W
S

D-house 5, elevations, plans, 1:400

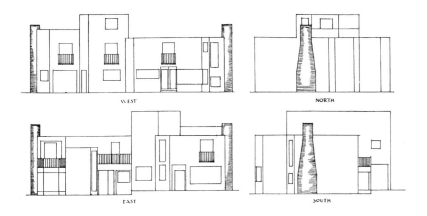

WEST

NORTH

EAST

SOUTH

## THE SIXTH D-HOUSE

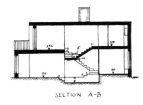

SECTION A-B

FIRST FLOOR

GROUND FLOOR

D-MANSION    GROCER'S HOME

## THE SIXTH D-HOUSE

In the sixth Double D-house, Frank has reverted to a more or less orthogonal plan, and its complexity is achieved through various spatial variations reminiscent of the houses from the 1920s and 1930s. The corners of most of the rooms in the section intended for Grill feature 45-degree angles. The result is that only the two bedrooms on the upper floor have right angles. This composition does not follow any obvious system, consisting rather of an almost random collection of different parts. Once again, Frank introduces several different levels in a manner that follows Loos' "Raumplan" principles.

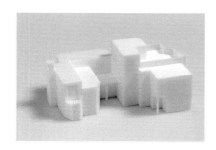

The sixth D-house, model

The sixth D-house, elevations, plans, section

The sixth D-house, watercolour

## CITY PLANS AND PROJECTS

*Sometime around 1950, Frank completed a number of urban planning projects for imaginary small towns. Frank here tests various combinations of street plans and exploitation levels. He combines narrower street spaces with open court-yard solutions and low-slung single-family houses. The starting point is a calculated diversity and variation that are directly connected to the ideas Frank expressed in his text "Accidentism".*

78          Town for 20.000 people, ca. 1950 (project)

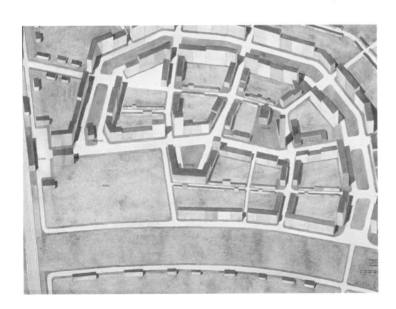

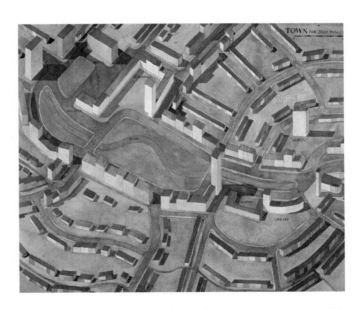

Town for 15.000 people, ca. 1950 (project)

Town for 2.000 families, ca. 1950 (project)

79

Project for a villa, 1955                    Round Stone House, mid-1950s (project)

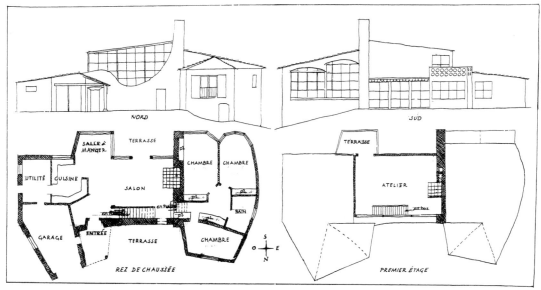

NORD

SUD

SALLE À MANGER

TERRASSE

CHAMBRE

CHAMBRE

TERRASSE

UTILITÉ

CUISINE

SALON

ATELIER

BAIN

GARAGE

ENTRÉE

TERRASSE

CHAMBRE

S
O · E
N

REZ DE CHAUSSÉE

PREMIER ÉTAGE

Project for a house for Trude Wæhner, Provence, late 1950s, elevations, plans

This is a project that involves a combined studio and home for Frank's good friend, the artist Trude Wæhner. The main structure of the house is composed of a number of apparently disparate parts: a curved and plastered chimney structure along with an entrance and garage, a red-painted glass section for the studio and the plaster con-

struction containing the bedrooms. Traditional architecture is combined with modern.

Inside the house, the internal relationship between the rooms is open and the rooms themselves feature irregular or curved walls.

Project for a house for Trude Wæhner, Provence, late 1950s, watercolour

## THE U.N. headquarters

It is not clear whether this was an actual competition entry for the UN headquarters or a private project.

A cluster of three slim high-rise structures standing next to each other is interconnected by pedestrian bridges (not unlike the Ponte dei Sospiri in Venice). Each high-rise building has a separate design and the shortest of the three is raised from the ground on pillars. Frank combines light modern glass facades with decorative elements that vary in each of the three buildings, creating a dialogue between the similar yet individual structures.

United Nations Headquarters, New York. Approx. 1947 (project)

The hotel project combines anonymous urban architecture with a varied and highly plastic hotel façade above street level. The angular bay windows contrast with the straight lines of the awnings. Frank uses the project as an illustration to his article on "Accidentism": "Hotel façade: the plasticity of the windows and balconies makes an inviting impression and distinguishes the building as a hotel."

Hotel at a boulevard, mid-1950s (project)

85

## FURNITURE AND FABRICS

*During the years Frank spent in exile in New York from 1942 to 1946, he created a multitude of fabric designs. To celebrate Estrid Ericson's 50th birthday in 1944, he sent her 50 new fabric designs.*

*After Frank returned to Stockholm in 1946, Svenskt Tenn kept him busy with numerous interior design commissions. During this period he also designed many new pieces of furniture, as well as lighting fixtures and decorative objets d'art.*

*Just as in his early furniture design work, Frank often based his pieces on traditional designs that he developed or distorted. He found inspiration in Biedermeier, as well as in Asian and in Nordic traditions.*

Table, designed ca. 1946

Chair and Armchair, designed 1947

Cabinet, designed 1946

Chest-of-Drawers, designed ca. 1950

Cabinet, designed 1957          Floor lamp, designed 1952          Cabinet, desigend 1954          89

Drinks, designed 1943-44

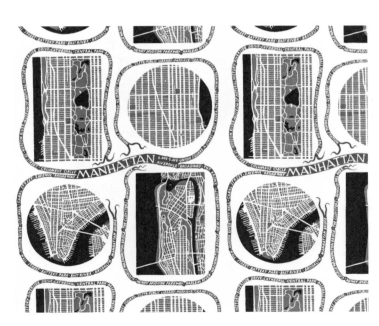

Manhattan, designed 1943-44

91

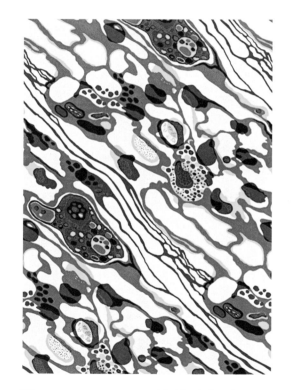

Marble, designed 1943-44

La Plata, designed 1943-44

Green Birds, designed 1943-44

Hawaii, designed 1943-44

Rox and Fix, designed 1943-44

Terazzo, designed 1943-44

THANKS TO:
Yvonne Sörensen, Svenskt Tenn, Stockholm
Kjell och Märta Beijers Stiftelse, Stockholm
Karin Winter, Arkitekturmuseet, Stockholm
Hermann Czech, Vienna